Recipes from Around the World

# $\mathscr{P}$AN-COOKED CHICKEN DISHES

IMP Limited

# CONTENTS

# CHICKEN DISHES FROM ALL OVER THE WORLD

*Chicken is versatile, economical and quick to cook so it's not surprising it's the most popular of all meats. It combines well with many different ingredients, from tangy citrus fruits and aromatic spices to creamy sauces and fiery chillies. Whether you eat it grilled with salad and baked potatoes, casseroled with Mediterranean vegetables or quickly stir-fried with exotic Asian flavours, you can be sure it'll always be finger-licking good.*

### Did you know?

Today's chickens are descendants of wild fowl from the Far East. Chicken is the most popular of all meats and no country's cuisine is complete without a whole range of chicken recipes.

### Did you know?

The best olives, an essential ingredient in many popular Mediterranean chicken dishes, are picked when they are absolutely dry and are not allowed to touch the ground so they keep their delicious aroma.

### Which Chicken Cut for Which Dish?

| Type of Cut | Used for | Cooking Times |
| --- | --- | --- |
| whole chicken | oven roasts | 20min per 450g/1lb + 20min |
| chicken quarters/portions | casseroles | 45min–1 hour |
| wings, drumsticks and thighs | fried or grilled as finger food; (deep-)fried with dips | 15–20min |
| breasts | cut into strips for stir-fries; grilled, fried, poached etc; stuffed; coated | 10–25min |
| minced chicken | chicken burgers | 10–15min |

### Did you know?

Tarragon, which is excellent with chicken, is one of the few herbs which probably originated in Europe. It was thought to protect anyone who ate it from dangerous animals and its name means 'little dragon'.

### Did you know?

It's maybe not to everyone's taste but Chicken Mole is a classic dish in Mexico. The sauce is made with many spices, nuts, dried fruits, chillies and ... bitter chocolate!

## SHOPPING TIPS

Chicken is available both fresh and frozen all year round. It tastes better the more naturally it has been raised: free-range birds, which roam outdoors and are fed on grain, have the finest flavour. Their skin colour will vary from off-white to golden yellow if fed on maize, but don't buy any with discoloured skin. When choosing pre-packed chicken, avoid any with excess liquid in the pack and check the best-before date. Supermarkets and butchers sell chicken ready-portioned so you can buy joints suitable for your recipe, whether legs, breasts or drumsticks. It's also worth remembering that a whole chicken is easy to cut up and often more economical too. For tips on portioning a chicken see page 60.

## STORAGE GUIDE

Put frozen chicken in the freezer as soon as you get home and only defrost it if you are cooking it straight away. Fresh chicken can be frozen if marked 'suitable for home freezing' on the packet. Do not freeze chicken for more than four months or its texture and flavour will deteriorate.

## HEALTH NOTES

Chicken is delicious, and equally popular with both children and adults. It is a very lean meat, containing less fat than even turkey or veal. If you are trying to lose weight or have to watch your cholesterol level, remove the skin before cooking as this contains most of the saturated fats.

## FOOD SAFETY

To reduce the dangers of food poisoning from harmful salmonella bacteria, follow these simple rules:
• Always thaw frozen whole chicken properly. It will need 24 hours in the fridge or eight hours at room temperature to defrost completely.
• Always ensure the chicken is cooked right through to the bone. When the thickest part of the flesh is pierced with a skewer, the juices must run clear, not pink.
• Wash your hands and utensils in hot water, and store raw chicken separately from cooked meat.

# FRUITY CHICKEN CURRY

**INDIA**

*Tender pieces of chicken in a creamy sauce flavoured with spices, ginger, fresh pineapple, juicy mango and roasted coconut – a dish fit for a king from the land of the maharajas.*

## INGREDIENTS
### (Serves 4)

- 4 chicken breasts, skinned and boned
- 1 tbsp plain flour
- salt and black pepper
- 1 mango
- ½ fresh pineapple
- 2.5cm/1in fresh ginger
- 3 shallots
- 2 tbsp vegetable oil or ghee
- 3 tsp curry powder
- 200ml/7fl oz chicken stock
- 100ml/4fl oz natural yoghurt
- 2 tbsp grated coconut
- fresh mint, to garnish

### INGREDIENTS TIP
Ghee is extremely popular in India and can be used instead of oil for frying. Essentially clarified butter, it can be heated to high temperatures, without burning.

1 Cut the chicken breasts into 1cm/½in strips. Mix the flour with the salt and pepper on a plate, add the chicken strips and toss until evenly coated.

2 Peel the mango, pineapple, ginger and shallots. Cut the mango flesh off the stone, core the pineapple and cut both fruit into bite-sized pieces. Finely chop the ginger and the shallots.

3 Heat the oil in a large frying pan or wok. Shake off any excess flour from the chicken and add the strips to the pan. Fry for 5 minutes over high heat or until browned. Remove from the pan with a slotted spoon and set aside.

4 Fry the shallots and ginger in the pan for 2 minutes. Add the fruit and curry powder and fry for 1 minute, stirring. Add chicken stock and bring to the boil. Turn down the heat and simmer for 5 minutes. Return the chicken and stir in the yoghurt. Season. Cover and simmer for 5 minutes.

5 Meanwhile, dry-fry the coconut in a frying pan over high heat. Sprinkle over the curry before serving. Garnish with mint.

**Step 1**

**Step 2**

**Step 4**

Preparation **20** Min Cooking **20** Min
Per Serving: 350 kcal/1466 kJ;
36g protein; 19g fat;
11g carbohydrate

## TYPICALLY INDIAN
No Indian feast would be complete without a chicken curry, especially in Kerala. This fertile region in south-west India, laced with lakes and rivers, is known as 'land of the coconuts'. Most people keep chickens, and as the region is blessed with an abundant fruit harvest, you often find the two used together in recipes.

## COOKING TIP

Most Indian cooks would not use curry powder,
preferring instead to blend their own special mix.
One advantage of ready-made curry powders is that
you can choose the heat you like. Whatever you use
though, all spices need to be fried first: this releases
all their pungent power to flavour the food.

## SERVING SUGGESTION

Serve with sour lime pickle, fragrant
basmati rice and poppadums or
puffy naan bread.

Serve with lassi: a mix of plain yogurt, iced
water, salt and ground cumin, or chilled lager.

# CHICKEN TIKKA MASALA

**INDIA**

*This recipe is an anglicised version of a traditional Indian tikka dish, popularised by the many Indian restaurants in the UK. It reflects the Indian love of aromatic, spicy food.*

## INGREDIENTS
### (Serves 4)

- 4 chicken breasts, skinned and boned
- 2 garlic cloves
- 2.5cm/1in fresh ginger
- 400g/14oz can chopped tomatoes
- 4 tbsp natural yoghurt
- 1 onion
- 2 tbsp vegetable oil
- 2 tbsp masala curry paste
- salt and black pepper
- 1 tbsp plain flour
- 50ml/2fl oz water
- 3 tbsp chopped fresh coriander
- coriander leaves, to garnish

### INGREDIENTS TIP

Ready-made jars of masala curry paste are available from most supermarkets. If you can't find fresh ginger, use 1 teaspoon of ground ginger.

1 Cut the chicken breasts into 2.5cm/1in cubes. Peel and roughly chop the garlic and ginger. Put the tomatoes, garlic, ginger and yoghurt into a blender or food processor and process until the mixture is smooth. Set aside.

Step 1

2 Peel and chop the onion. Heat the oil in a heavy-based pan, add the onion and fry over a medium heat for 3–4 minutes, stirring constantly.

3 Stir in the masala curry paste and fry for a further 1 minute over a medium heat, stirring once or twice.

Step 3

4 Add the tomato mixture and chicken to the pan and mix together. Season with salt and pepper. Mix the flour and water together and stir into the pan off the heat. Return to the heat and bring to the boil, stirring constantly. Cover and cook over a gentle heat for 15 minutes. Sprinkle in the chopped coriander and serve immediately garnished with coriander leaves.

Step 4

Preparation **20** Min Cooking **20** Min
Per Serving: 282 kcal/1182 kJ;
35g protein; 14g fat;
5g carbohydrate

## TYPICALLY INDIAN
In India cooks buy whole spices from their local markets and then grind the pods and seeds with a pestle in a mortar to make their own preferred curry blend. The spices are displayed in the market in small sacks and give off a wonderfully spicy aroma.

SERVING SUGGESTION Accompany with pilau basmati rice, mango chutney, raita and poppadums.

Serve with tea, mineral water or an Indian beer such as Cobra.

**SERVING SUGGESTION** Serve with either lime pickle or a tangy mango chutney. Offer green tea or a cooling glass of fresh fruit juice, such as mango or passion fruit.

# SINGAPORE FRIED NOODLES

**SINGAPORE**

*This classic dish from Singapore is a colourful combination of tender chicken strips and tofu, tossed with hot chillies and spring onions in a fragrant coconut sauce.*

## INGREDIENTS
### (Serves 4)

- 50g/2oz cashew nuts
- 1 tbsp coriander seeds
- 1 tbsp cumin seeds
- 2 tsp chilli powder
- 4 tbsp groundnut oil
- 400ml/14fl oz canned coconut milk
- 150g/5oz rice noodles
- 3 chicken breasts, skinned and boned
- 1 red and 1 green chilli
- 1 bunch spring onions
- 3 tomatoes
- 100g/4oz tofu
- salt and black pepper
- fresh coriander, to garnish

### INGREDIENTS TIP
Use dried egg noodles (sold in compressed squares) instead of the rice noodles.

1 Put the cashew nuts, coriander seeds, cumin and chilli powder in a food processor and blend until ground. Heat half the oil in a frying pan and fry the mixture for 1 minute. Stir in the coconut milk, bring to the boil and simmer for 6 minutes.

**Step 1**

2 Place the rice noodles in a bowl, cover with boiling water and leave to stand for 2–3 minutes. Drain. Cut the chicken into strips. Core and de-seed the chillies and chop. Diagonally slice the spring onions and roughly chop the tomatoes. Drain the tofu and cut into dice.

**Step 2**

3 Heat the remaining oil in a wok or frying pan and stir-fry the chicken for 5 minutes, or until browned. Add the chillies and spring onions and stir-fry for 2 minutes.

**Step 3**

4 Add the roughly chopped tomatoes, the diced tofu, the noodles and coconut mixture to the pan and stir-fry for another 2 minutes, or until the whole thing is heated through. Season to taste with salt and pepper. Roughly chop the fresh coriander and sprinkle over the dish to serve.

Preparation **20** Min Cooking **18** Min
Per Serving: 596 kcal/2481 kJ;
33g protein; 44g fat;
18g carbohydrate

## TYPICALLY ORIENTAL
Just as its modern culture seems in complete contrast to its ancient roots, the cuisine of Singapore is equally as surprising and diverse. With contributions from China, India and Malaysia the food is an exciting and eclectic mix of styles and flavours.

*Asia & The Far East* **11**

# CHICKEN TERIYAKI

**JAPAN**

## INGREDIENTS
(Serves 4)

- 4 chicken breasts, boned
- 2 small leeks
- 4 tbsp sake or dry sherry
- 4 tbsp mirin or Marsala
- 3 tbsp caster sugar
- 5 tbsp dark soy sauce
- 1 tbsp vegetable oil

**TO GARNISH**
- radishes, cucumbers and spring onions

### INGREDIENTS TIP

If you want to use authentic Japanese ingredients, both sake (rice wine) and mirin (sweet rice wine) can be found in oriental super-markets. However, dry sherry and Marsala or sweet sherry make excellent substitutes.

*A favourite way of cooking meat and poultry in Japan. This version is made with chicken, crisply fried then simmered in a sticky sauce and served garnished with decorative vegetables.*

1 Make three diagonal cuts into the skin of the chicken. Trim the leeks, wash thoroughly and cut into 4cm/1½in pieces.

2 Heat a non-stick frying pan over high heat. Add the chicken breasts, skin side down and fry for 3 minutes. Turn over and fry for a further 4 minutes. Remove the chicken from the pan and discard any fat.

Step 1

3 In the same pan, bring the sake or sherry, mirin or Marsala and sugar to the boil, stirring until the sugar has dissolved. Return the chicken to the pan, cover and simmer for 2 minutes. Add the soy sauce, bring back to the boil, cover and cook over high heat for 6 minutes, turning the chicken occasionally, until the sauce thickens.

4 Transfer the chicken to a warmed plate. Discard the sauce. Heat the oil in another frying pan and fry the leeks for 3 minutes until softened.

Step 3

5 Cut the chicken into thick slices and fan out onto warmed serving plates. Arrange the leeks on the plates. Cut the radishes, cucumber and spring onions into decorative shapes and use to garnish the dish.

Step 5

Preparation **10** Min Cooking **25** Min
Per Serving: 306 kcal/1284 kJ;
35g protein; 9g fat;
3g carbohydrate

## TYPICALLY JAPANESE

Eating plays a large part in the Land of the Rising Sun. The Japanese attach great importance to the freshness and quality of ingredients which must look beautiful when served. Foods are prepared so their natural flavours remain unmasked, and thus are often served elaborately garnished.

## COOKING TIPS

It is important to cook the chicken skin-side down over a really high heat as this produces nice crispy skin and it also makes the fat run • If you prefer, instead of discarding the thickened sauce, you can spoon it into a small bowl and serve it at the table as a dipping sauce.

## SERVING SUGGESTIONS

Serve a salad of grated white cabbage, carrots and cucumber or just a bowl of boiled rice and vegetables.

Serve with one of the new Japanese beers or a light white wine such as Sancerre.

13

# THAI RED CHICKEN CURRY

**THAILAND**

## INGREDIENTS
### (Serves 4)

- 400ml/14fl oz canned coconut milk
- 3 tbsp red Thai curry paste, or to taste
- 4 chicken breasts, skinned and boned
- 4 tbsp fish sauce or soy sauce
- 2 tbsp caster sugar
- 225g/8oz canned bamboo shoots in brine
- 1 medium-sized aubergine
- juice of 1 lime
- fresh basil leaves
- 1 tbsp grated fresh coconut

### INGREDIENTS TIP
Red and green Thai curry pastes are available from all supermarkets. If you can find them, use 5 lime leaves instead of the basil leaves for a more authentic flavour.

*Thai cuisine relies on aromatic ingredients such as coconut and lime leaves for its characteristic flavour. In this classic dish the chicken is simmered in a fragrant red curry sauce.*

1 Pour 200ml/7fl oz of the canned coconut milk into a large saucepan. Stir in the red Thai curry paste and bring the mixture to the boil. Boil rapidly for 4 minutes or until the sauce is reduced by half.

Step 2

2 Using a sharp knife, cut the chicken breasts into 2.5cm/1in pieces. Add to the coconut sauce in the pan and bring back to the boil. Reduce the heat to low and simmer the chicken for 5 minutes, stirring now and again.

3 Stir in the fish sauce or soy sauce and the sugar and bring back to the boil. Drain the bamboo shoots and cut into matchsticks. Cut the aubergine into small chunks. Add to the pan with the bamboo shoots. Bring up to the boil again, lower the heat and simmer for about 5 minutes.

Step 3

4 Stir in the remaining canned coconut milk, lime juice and 2 tablespoons shredded basil leaves. Heat through for another 2–3 minutes. Spoon the curry into a serving dish and serve sprinkled with more basil leaves and the grated fresh coconut.

Step 4

Preparation **15** Min Cooking **20** Min
Per Serving: 490 kcal/2044 kJ;
37g protein; 33g fat; 12g carbohydrate

## TYPICALLY THAI
Good food is always important in Thailand, whether it's for a religious festival or a farmer's midday meal. Stir-frying is one of the most popular methods of cooking, more so because a stir-fry can be set up on a fire and cooked anywhere – on a street corner, next to the paddy fields or even on the roadside.

## Cooking tips

Thai cuisine is renowned for mixing hot, sour, sweet and salty flavours; it is a very versatile way of cooking so you can add more or less of any ingredient to accentuate the flavours you like the best * If you prefer a runnier sauce then reduce the coconut milk by one third instead of one half at the beginning of the recipe.

## Serving suggestion

Serve with noodles, sauces and seasonings: chillies in fish sauce, chillies in vinegar, sugar and lime wedges.

 Serve with iced tea, lager or a chilled white wine.

# 3 WAYS WITH CHICKEN STIR-FRY

*Stir-frying is one of the most popular ways of cooking in the Far East and is a healthy way to make a quick meal. Here chicken is fried with basic ingredients, then different flavourings are added.*

## BASIC STIR-FRY

**(SERVES 4)**
- 4 chicken breasts, skinned and boned
- 2 garlic cloves
- 1cm/½in fresh ginger
- 1 bunch spring onions
- 2 tbsp vegetable oil

*Easily prepared in minutes, this basic recipe can be adapted to make three delicious dishes.*

**1** Using a sharp knife, cut the chicken breasts into thick strips, 4cm/1½in long.

**2** Finely chop or crush the garlic cloves. Peel the ginger and cut into pieces the size of matchsticks. Trim the spring onions and thickly slice on the diagonal.

**3** Heat the oil in a wok over high heat until almost smoking. Add the ginger and garlic and stir-fry for 1 minute. Add the chicken and stir-fry for a further 5 minutes, until browned. Add the spring onions and stir-fry for 1 minute.

## SWEET & SOUR CHICKEN STIR-FRY

Preparation **15** Min Cooking **10** Min

### CHINA

- 225g/8oz canned water chestnuts
- 2 carrots
- 3 tbsp soy sauce
- 1 tbsp sherry
- 2 tbsp tomato purée
- 2 tbsp rice wine vinegar
- pinch of sugar

**4** Drain the water chestnuts and cut in half. Peel and cut the carrots into matchsticks. Add to the wok with the spring onions and stir-fry for 1 minute.

**5** Mix the rest of the ingredients together. Add to wok and stir-fry for 30 seconds. Garnish with shredded spring onions if liked.

# CHICKEN & COCONUT
## STIR-FRY

Preparation **15** Min Cooking **10** Min

### INDONESIA

- 1 stem lemon grass
- 100g/4oz peanuts
- 400ml/14fl oz can coconut milk
- 4 tbsp oyster sauce
- 3 tbsp fresh chopped coriander
- salt
- lime wedges

**4** Finely shred lemon grass. Add to wok with peanuts while stir-frying vegetables. Add coconut milk after stir-frying chicken. Bring to boil, simmer 1 minute.

**5** Continue with basic recipe. Stir in oyster sauce, most of coriander and salt. Garnish with lime and coriander.

# CHICKEN & FRESH
## HERB STIR-FRY

Preparation **15** Min Cooking **10** Min

### VIETNAM

- 1 tbsp sesame oil
- 2 tbsp fish sauce or soy sauce
- 2 tbsp sherry
- 4 tbsp each chopped fresh mint and coriander
- 225g/8oz beansprouts
- iceberg lettuce
- cucumber slices

**4** Mix the sesame oil, fish or soy sauce, sherry, and most of the chopped fresh mint and coriander together.

**5** Stir this sauce into the stir-fry with the beansprouts and heat through. Arrange a few whole large lettuce leaves on plates and spoon the stir-fry into them. Garnish with the reserved herbs and the cucumber.

17

# $\mathscr{H}$ONEY & MUSTARD CHICKEN SALAD

*This fresh tasting salad of tender chicken and mouth-watering melon tossed in a sweet mustard dressing makes a great starter too, served in smaller portions.*

## INGREDIENTS
### (Serves 4)

- ½ Galia melon
- 2 kiwi fruit
- 2 tsp prepared English mustard
- 1 tbsp wholegrain mustard
- 2 tsp runny honey
- 1 tbsp lemon juice or white wine vinegar
- 5 tbsp olive oil
- 4 chicken breasts, skinned and boned
- 1 garlic clove
- salt and black pepper
- mixed salad leaves

### INGREDIENTS TIP

Try using a canteloupe or honeydew melon instead of the Galia. Or, for a spectacular splash of colour, add a few bright pink watermelon balls as well.

1 Cut the melon in half and discard the seeds. Using a melon baller, scoop out the flesh. Peel the kiwi fruit, cut in half lengthways and slice.

2 For the dressing, whisk both the English and wholegrain mustards, honey and lemon juice or wine vinegar together. Whisk in 2 tablespoons oil and season with salt and pepper.

3 Using a sharp knife, cut the chicken breasts into 1cm/½in cubes. Heat the remaining oil in a pan and fry the chicken over moderate heat for 8 minutes until browned and tender. Remove the pan from the heat. Crush the garlic, stir into the chicken and season with salt and pepper.

4 Put the chicken, the melon balls, kiwi fruit and the dressing into a large bowl. Toss together so everything is well coated in dressing. Taste and adjust the seasoning. Arrange the salad leaves on serving plates and spoon the chicken salad over the top.

Step 1

Step 2

Step 3

Preparation **25** Min Cooking **8** Min
Per Serving: 383 kcal/1599 kJ;
34g protein; 25g fat;
7g carbohydrate

## TYPICALLY AUSTRALIAN

Most of the population of Australia live around the coast and enjoy an enviable climate. Not surprisingly, barbecues have become the nation's favourite way of eating. Chargrilled meat, poultry and seafood served with tempting crisp salads are a speciality.

## COOKING TIPS

To enhance the flavour of the salad, cook the chicken in advance then toss in the dressing while still warm (without the fruit). Cover and leave to marinate overnight in the fridge • If you like onions, add ½ chopped red onion to the salad. Red onions are sweeter than white and less overpowering.

## SERVING SUGGESTION

Serve a cooling scoop or two of rich nutty ice cream with bought or homemade chocolate sauce.

🍷 A chilled Australian Chardonnay
   will go well with the salad.

# $\mathscr{S}$PICY CHICKEN & RICE

USA

*A hearty chicken stew from the Southern States, made of peppers, juicy fresh tomatoes and rice. The dash of Tabasco at the end adds the authentic Louisiana taste.*

## INGREDIENTS
### (Serves 4)

- 1.5kg/3lb chicken
- 1 red, 1 green and 1 yellow pepper
- 2 green chillies
- 450g/1lb tomatoes
- 1 onion
- 2 tbsp vegetable oil
- salt and cayenne pepper
- 1 tsp paprika
- 150g/5oz long grain rice
- 450ml/¾ pint hot vegetable stock
- 1 tsp dried thyme
- 100g/4oz green olives
- few drops of Tabasco
- 2 tbsp shredded flat leaf parsley

## INGREDIENTS TIP

The heat of a chilli depends on its variety. Colour is only an indication of ripeness: green chillies are harvested unripe, whereas red are ripe.

1 Cut the chicken into 12 pieces. Cut the peppers and chillies in half, then remove the seeds and white pith. Cut the peppers into quarters and finely chop the chillies. Make a few cuts in the tomatoes, put into a bowl, pour over boiling water and leave for a few minutes. Peel off the skin and chop the flesh. Dice the onion.

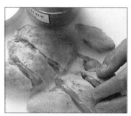

Step 1

2 Heat the oil in a large frying pan. Season the chicken with salt and cayenne, add to the pan and fry for 8 minutes, turning to brown all over. Remove the chicken from the pan. Add the peppers and onion and fry for 5 minutes until browned. Remove from the pan with a slotted spoon. Add the chillies, paprika and rice and fry, stirring for 1 minute, to coat the rice in oil.

Step 2

3 Add the hot vegetable stock to the pan, cover and cook the rice over low heat for 10 minutes. Return the peppers, onion and chicken to the pan, add the thyme and tomatoes, cover and simmer for 20 minutes.

4 Stone the olives if necessary, roughly chop and stir into the pan. Add the Tabasco, then taste and add seasoning. Sprinkle with parsley and serve.

Step 4

Preparation **30** Min Cooking **45** Min
Per Serving: 575kcal/1839 kJ;
30g protein; 18g fat;
42g carbohydrate

## TYPICALLY AMERICAN

Louisiana is the home of Tabasco sauce, which is still produced by the McIllhenny family on Avery Island. Like the wild poultry the first immigrants lived on, Tabasco is also a 'native' product. It uses local ingredients – chillies and salt from the local salt mine – which are simply left to ferment.

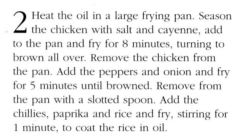

## COOKING TIP

Stock can be as easy as removing the cube from its wrapper, but homemade vegetable stock has a much better flavour. Brown chopped turnips, carrots, celery and onion in oil very slowly – about 30 minutes. Add the onion skins, parsley, bay leaves, garlic and thyme and cover with water. Simmer for 3 hours, then strain.

## SERVING SUGGESTION

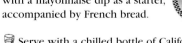

Serve deep-fried breaded prawns with a mayonnaise dip as a starter, accompanied by French bread.

 Serve with a chilled bottle of Californian Chardonnay or Sauvignon Blanc.

SERVING SUGGESTION Serve with coconut
rice: simmer rice in coconut milk instead of water.

Serve with a fresh fruit punch: leave for a few
hours to develop its flavour and serve ice cold.

# CREOLE CHICKEN WITH PINEAPPLE

**TRINIDAD**

## INGREDIENTS

(Serves 4)

- 1.5kg/3lb chicken
- salt and black pepper
- 3 tbsp lemon juice
- 3 spring onions
- 4 celery stalks
- 2 green chillies
- ½ pineapple
- 1 banana
- 40g/1½oz butter
- a few drops of Tabasco
- fresh coriander sprigs
- 150ml/¼ pint chicken stock

INGREDIENTS TIP

If fresh pineapples are out of season, simply use a can: you will need about 425g/15oz drained pineapple. In Trinidad, they would use plantains which are larger than bananas, with a firm, starchy flesh. Buy bananas that are not fully ripe for the right consistency.

*An unbeatable combination of sweet, hot and sour ingredients, this is Caribbean cooking at its best. The fruity flavours of pineapple and banana, chillies and lemon are perfect together.*

1 Cut the chicken into 12 pieces, then season well with salt, black pepper and 2 tablespoons of the lemon juice.

2 Trim the spring onions and chop. Trim the celery and cut into slices, reserving some of the leaves. Cut the chillies in half, remove the seeds and white pith and dice. Peel the pineapple, remove the core and cut into bite-sized pieces. Chop the banana and mash to a purée with the rest of the lemon juice.

3 Melt the butter in a large pan. Add the chicken and fry for 10 minutes or until golden. Remove from the pan. Add the prepared vegetables and pineapple to the pan and fry for 3 minutes until softened and browned. Add the banana purée and return the chicken to the pan, season with salt, pepper and Tabasco.

4 Separate the coriander leaves from the stems. Put some leaves aside for garnishing, finely chop the rest and add to the pan, together with the chicken stock. Bring to the boil, cover then simmer for 30 minutes, or until tender. Serve garnished with the reserved celery leaves and the coriander.

Step 3

Step 3

Step 4

Preparation **30** Min Cooking **45** Min
Per Serving: 292 kcal/1218 kJ;
25g protein; 16g fat;
12g carbohydrate

TYPICALLY CREOLE

Locally-grown fruit like bananas and pineapples are often used in stews in Trinidad. Neither fruit is native to the area though – the pineapple found its way into the Caribbean via Africa, and the banana started its journey from Asia around 650 AD.

# CARIBBEAN CHICKEN

**JAMAICA**

*These crispy fried chicken pieces are cooked with all the favourite flavours of the Caribbean – smooth dark rum, fragrant coconut and luscious aromatic mango.*

## INGREDIENTS
(Serves 4)

- 2 garlic cloves
- salt
- 3 limes
- 2 tbsp mango juice (see Cooking Tip)
- 100ml/4fl oz dark rum
- 1.5kg/3lb chicken
- 2 tbsp grated fresh or desiccated coconut
- 175g/6oz plain flour
- 2 eggs
- oil for deep-fat frying

### TO GARNISH
- 1 ripe mango

## INGREDIENTS TIP

Desiccated coconut is a good substitute for fresh. Alternatively finely chop, or grind, peanuts or cashew nuts to make a delicious coating for the chicken.

1 Peel the garlic, sprinkle with salt and crush with a fork. Squeeze the juice of 1 lime and mash it into the garlic with the mango juice and rum.

2 Cut the chicken into 12 pieces. Put into a bowl and pour over the marinade. Cover the bowl, put into the fridge and marinate for 1 hour, turning the pieces now and again.

Step 1

3 Mix the grated coconut with half the flour. Put the rest of the flour on another plate. Beat the eggs. Remove the chicken from the marinade. Dip first in plain flour, then egg and finally coconut flour. Heat the oil in a large frying pan (see Cooking Tip).

Step 3

4 Fry the chicken in three batches for about 15 minutes each, turning once, until golden; fry the chicken breasts for 12 minutes only. Put the chicken on a plate lined with kitchen paper towels and keep warm in a low oven.

5 Cut the rest of the limes into slices. Cut the mango into very thin wedges. Garnish the chicken with the fruit.

Step 4

Preparation **30** Min
Marinating **1** Hour Frying **45** Min
Per Serving: 590 kcal/2463 kJ;
36g protein; 31g fat;
31g carbohydrate

## TYPICALLY JAMAICAN
Along with music, it is claimed that eating is one of the most popular pastimes in the Caribbean. It's no surprise therefore that their exotic cuisine has influenced the islands' dancing habits: rhythmic dances are named after famous dishes like 'salsa' meaning sauce, or 'merengue' meaning sweet meringue.

## Cooking tips

Make sure the oil is at the right temperature for frying, that is 180°C/350°F (use a thermometer to check). If the oil is any hotter, the coconut coating will burn • For the mango juice, prepare the mango at the start and save the juice. If the mango isn't ripe enough, use fresh orange juice.

## Serving suggestion

Serve with a salad of carrot, courgette, avocado, tomato and oak-leaf lettuce.

 Chill tumblers and fill with ice-cold sparkling water flavoured with a dash of lime juice.

# CHICKEN MEXICANA

**MEXICO**

*Succulent chicken breasts are simmered with tomato, crisp peppers and chillies and finished with a generous topping of grated cheese that melts into the tasty sauce.*

## INGREDIENTS

(Serves 4)

- 1 beefsteak tomato
- 2 onions
- 2 garlic cloves
- 75g/3oz walnut pieces
- 1 green and 1 red pepper
- 2 green chillies
- 2 tbsp vegetable oil
- 4 chicken breasts, skinned and boned
- salt and cayenne pepper
- 300ml/½ pint chicken stock
- 1 tsp chilli sauce
- 1-2 tbsp white wine vinegar
- 75g/3oz hard cheese, such as Cheddar

### INGREDIENTS TIP

In Mexico – and the United States as well – Monterey Jack is the most popular hard cheese and would be used in this recipe.

**1** Make a few cuts in the tomato, put into a bowl and pour over boiling water. Leave for a few minutes then peel. Roughly chop the tomato and set aside. Peel and chop the onions and purée with the garlic and walnuts in a food processor.

Step 1

**2** Cut the peppers and chillies in half and remove the seeds and white pith. Cut the peppers into chunks and the chillies into thin strips. Heat the oil in a large pan, add the chicken breasts and fry over high heat for 5 minutes on each side, or until golden brown. Remove from the pan and season with salt and cayenne.

Step 2

**3** Add the tomato, peppers, onion purée and chillies to the pan and pour in the chicken stock. Slowly bring to the boil, then season with chilli sauce, vinegar, salt and more cayenne. Reduce the heat to moderately low, put the chicken on top, cover the pan and simmer for 20 minutes.

Step 4

**4** Grate the cheese coarsely, remove the lid from the pan and sprinkle the cheese over the chicken breasts. Cover the pan again, turn off the heat and leave for 5 minutes or so, until the cheese has melted.

Preparation **40** Min Cooking **35** Min
Per Serving: 467 kcal/2884 kJ;
41g protein; 32g fat;
4g carbohydrate

## TYPICALLY MEXICAN

Mexicans love poultry and it forms the basis of many national dishes. Invading Spanish *conquistadores* brought chickens to South America and they returned home to Europe with the native Mexican turkey. Turkeys have always been popular, even in Aztec times: the Aztecs even kept them as pets!

## COOKING TIPS

If you prefer a slightly thinner sauce, don't bother puréeing the onions, garlic and walnuts, just add them to the pan with the peppers and chillies • Chillies contain *capsaicin*, the substance responsible for all that fiery flavour. Wash your hands after handling and don't touch your face or eyes.

## SERVING SUGGESTION

Serve with a crisp salad of cos lettuce, pine nuts and shaved Parmesan tossed in a mustard flavoured French dressing.

 Offer ice-cold beer in the bottle, with a wedge of lime tucked into its neck in the Mexican way.

# CHICKEN ENCHILADAS

## INGREDIENTS
### (Serves 4)

- 4 chicken breasts, skinned and boned
- 3 tbsp olive oil
- 400g/14oz can tomatoes
- ½ Spanish onion
- 2 garlic cloves
- 2 tsp chilli powder
- 1 tsp dried marjoram
- 300ml/½ pint chicken stock
- salt and black pepper
- 8 soft flour tortillas
- ½ Webbs lettuce
- 2 spring onions
- 75g/3oz feta cheese
- 1 red onion
- fresh coriander sprigs
- 1 lime or lemon

## INGREDIENTS TIP

You can use crisp U-shaped tacos instead of tortillas. Warm in the oven, then brush the insides with the sauce.

*A whole host of delicious ingredients goes into making these tasty enchiladas – cheese, lettuce, two types of onion and, of course, moist chunks of chicken.*

1 Cut the chicken breasts into strips. Heat 2 tablespoons of the oil in a pan, add the chicken and stir-fry for 5 minutes, or until cooked. Using a slotted spoon, remove the chicken from the pan and keep warm.

2 Drain the tomatoes. Peel and finely chop the onion and garlic. Heat the rest of the oil in the pan and fry the onion and garlic for 3 minutes. Add the tomatoes, chilli powder, marjoram and chicken stock and bring to the boil. Boil rapidly for 15 minutes, stirring now and again, or until the sauce is reduced by one third. Season to taste.

3 Wrap the tortillas in foil and bake in a 180°C/350°F/gas 4 oven for 10 minutes. Meanwhile, shred the lettuce and the spring onions. Dice the feta cheese, then peel and finely slice the red onion.

4 Brush one side of each tortilla with the sauce. Scatter the lettuce and chicken on top. Working quickly, roll up the tortillas and arrange on a serving plate. Spoon over the remaining sauce. Scatter cheese and onions over the tortillas. Garnish with coriander, and the lime or lemon cut into wedges.

Step 4

Step 4

Step 4

Preparation **20** Min Cooking **25** Min
Per Serving: 746 kcal/3148 kJ;
52g protein; 22g fat;
91g carbohydrate

## TYPICALLY MEXICAN

Mexicans enjoy eating outdoors and throughout Mexico roadside stalls sell all kinds of appetising morsels. There is usually grilled corn on the cob and always tortillas, served in many different ways. Rolled they are *enchiladas*, stuffed they become *burritos*, and *quesadillas* when made into little pies.

28 *Central & South America*

## COOKING TIP

It is easy to make tortillas yourself: combine 100g/4oz wholewheat flour, 5 tablespoons oil, 1 teaspoon salt and 100ml/4fl oz water (you may need a little more water). Knead, cover and leave to rest for 1 hour. Divide into walnut-sized pieces, roll out into thin pancakes and dry fry in a hot pan for 30–60 seconds.

## SERVING SUGGESTION

Serve with guacamole (spicy avocado dip) and a generous dollop of sour cream on the top.

Serve iced tomato juice, well-seasoned with Tabasco, or ice-cold Mexican lager.

# SPICED RICE CHICKEN PARCELS

**LEBANON**

*Bring a taste of the Middle East to your table with these chicken parcels, marinated in honey and filled with an exotic stuffing of rice, spices and dried fruit.*

## INGREDIENTS

(Serves 4)

- 5 tbsp vegetable oil
- 2 tbsp runny honey
- 2 tbsp lemon juice
- 1 tsp curry powder
- 4 chicken breasts, skinned and boned
- 2 tbsp pine nuts
- 50g/2oz sultanas
- 50g/2oz no-soak dried apricots
- 100g/4oz cooked long grain rice
- 1 pinch each ground allspice, cinnamon and cloves
- salt and pepper

### INGREDIENTS TIP

Allspice is also called pimento (not to be confused with pimiento which is a red pepper). This wonderful spice tastes and smells like a mixture of nutmeg, cinnamon and cloves, hence its name.

1 In a small bowl, mix 1 tablespoon of the oil with the honey, the lemon juice and the curry powder.

2 Using a small sharp knife, carefully cut a pocket in each of the chicken breasts. Put the chicken breasts in a dish, pour over the honey mixture and turn to coat. Set aside while you make the filling.

3 For the filling, dry-fry the pine nuts in a small pan for 1 minute, or until golden, stirring all the time. Finely chop the sultanas and apricots and place in a bowl. Add the rice, pine nuts, allspice, cinnamon and cloves and mix thoroughly. Season with salt and pepper to taste.

4 Carefully spoon the rice filling into the pockets in the chicken breasts. Close up and secure with cocktail sticks. Season the outside with salt and pepper.

5 Heat the remaining oil in a large frying pan and fry the stuffed chicken breasts for about 6–8 minutes on each side, or until golden and cooked through. Serve the chicken straight away.

Step 3

Step 4

Step 4

Preparation **45** Min Cooking **15** Min
Per Serving: 508 kcal/2125 kJ;
36g protein; 29g fat;
27g carbohydrate

## TYPICALLY LEBANESE

During the hot dry summers in the Lebanon, everyone has a constant thirst to quench. Little carts selling cooling iced lemonade and other fruit-based drinks are a welcome sight in these sweltering months. They stop on the roadside then move on, wheeled through the streets, to the next busy pitch.

## COOKING TIPS

You can use leftover rice for the filling, but make sure it is rice you cooked the day before. Any longer and the rice is past its best • Spices also deteriorate if stored for too long – buy in small quantities and keep in a dark, dry cupboard.

## SERVING SUGGESTION

The Lebanese love rich, sweet desserts: try baklava made from filo pastry layered with honey, nuts and spices.

 Finish with cinnamon tea: boil 1 cup water with 1 cinnamon stick per person. Sweeten to taste.

# MOROCCAN CHICKEN WITH HONEY

**MOROCCO**

*A fabulous Moroccan speciality, this chicken dish has a unique sweet-and-sour flavour, enhanced by a wonderful trio of traditional spices – turmeric, saffron and ginger.*

## INGREDIENTS
### (Serves 4)

- 1.5kg/3lb chicken
- 2 oranges
- 1 lemon
- 3 tbsp runny honey
- 1 onion
- 1 garlic clove
- 3 tbsp olive oil
- 300ml/½ pint hot chicken stock
- ½ tsp turmeric
- ½ tsp saffron powder
- ½ tsp ground ginger
- salt and black pepper
- 100g/4oz stoned black olives, optional

### INGREDIENTS TIP
Saffron is the most expensive of all spices. This is because it takes about 200,000 hand-picked saffron crocus stamens to produce just 450g/1lb of the spice.

1 Cut the chicken into 8 pieces and put into a large shallow bowl. Squeeze the juice of one of the oranges and the lemon into a small bowl and stir in the honey.

2 Pour the fruit juice and honey over the chicken pieces and toss to coat all over. Cover the bowl and leave at room temperature for 1 hour, turning the pieces now and again.

3 Peel and finely chop the onion and garlic. Remove the chicken from the marinade and reserve. Heat the oil in a large pan, add the onion and garlic and fry for 10 minutes over low heat. Add the chicken and fry for 10 minutes over moderately high heat.

4 Add the chicken stock and 2 tablespoons of the reserved marinade. Add the turmeric, saffron, ginger, salt and pepper. Bring to the boil, reduce the heat to low, cover and simmer for 45 minutes.

5 Peel and segment the other orange, leaving behind all the white pith and membranes. Transfer the chicken to a serving bowl and garnish with the orange and the black olives.

**Step 1**

**Step 2**

**Step 5**

---

Preparation **25** Min
Marinating **1** Hour
Cooking **1** Hour **5** Min
Per Serving: 496 kcal/2065 kJ;
40g protein; 35g fat;
11g carbohydrate

### TYPICALLY MOROCCAN
Spices are very important in Arabic cuisine: saffron, cinnamon, ginger, aniseed, coriander and cardamom make vivid displays on sale in the bazaars. All these spices are used in everyday Moroccan cooking. Combine their fabulous flavours with olive oil, garlic and lemon and you have the taste of Morocco.

## COOKING TIPS

You can use saffron strands instead of ground saffron. Soak a pinch of strands in 3 tablespoons hot water for 30 minutes. Add water and strands    Use a small, very sharp filleting knife to segment the oranges. Anything else will turn the flesh into a mush. Carefully cut down between each membrane and the segments will easily fall out.

## SERVING SUGGESTION

Serve with raisin rice: fry raisins briefly with rice in oil, then cook the rice in stock instead of water.

 Freshly made mint tea, sweetened with sugar or honey, rounds off the meal nicely.

33

**SERVING SUGGESTION** Offer pitta bread or couscous, another staple of North African cuisine.

Serve with a jug of mineral water with added ice cubes and lemon or lime wedges.

# CHICKEN TAGINE

**INGREDIENTS**
(Serves 4)

- 1.5kg/3lb chicken
- 3 onions
- 50g/2oz butter
- 1 tsp saffron powder
- ½ tsp ground ginger
- 1 tbsp paprika
- ¼ tsp ground cinnamon
- 100g/4oz dates, stoned
- 275g/10oz frozen broad beans, thawed
- salt and black pepper
- fresh coriander sprigs
- fresh parsley sprigs

## INGREDIENTS TIP

If you prefer, remove the outer skins from the broad beans, before cooking, to make them more tender. Instead of broad beans add a can of chick peas to the chicken mixture.

*This North African dish is named after the earthenware pot it is traditionally cooked in. Here chicken is simmered with the traditional flavourings of sweet spices and dried fruit.*

1 Cut the chicken into 12 pieces. Put the chicken into a large, heavy-based saucepan with a tight-fitting lid.

2 Peel and chop one of the onions into thin rings and finely chop the other two onions. Add the onion rings to the chicken in the pan with the butter. Pour in about 450ml/¾ pint cold water, or just enough to cover the chicken.

Step 2

3 Bring slowly to the boil, reduce the heat to low, cover the pan and simmer gently for about 30 minutes.

4 Add the saffron, ginger, paprika, cinnamon, finely chopped onions, the dates and broad beans to the chicken. Stir well, put the lid back on and simmer for another 30 minutes.

Step 4

5 Taste the liquid and season with salt and black pepper. Transfer the chicken to a serving dish, or if you have one, a classic tagine dish. Roughly chop the fresh herbs and sprinkle over the finished dish. Add a few parsley sprigs to garnish.

Step 5

Preparation **30** Min Cooking **1** Hour
Per Serving: 362 kcal/1511 kJ;
31g protein; 16g fat;
24g carbohydrate

## TYPICALLY MOROCCAN

The Arabs, or the 'sons of the desert', still roam the often hostile and barren countryside from one oasis to another, together with their herds of cattle. Beef has always been their staple diet and meals nearly always contain meat, flavoured with dried fruit and spices.

# CHICKEN KIEV

**UKRAINE**

*A Ukrainian speciality from the city of Kiev. The crunchy coated chicken breasts are filled with a knob of garlic and herb butter which helps keep the meat moist and succulent.*

## INGREDIENTS

(Serves 4)

- 4 chicken breasts, skinned and boned
- 4 garlic cloves
- 1 lemon
- 1 tbsp chopped fresh mixed herbs, eg parsley, dill, chives or 1 tsp dried mixed herbs
- salt and black pepper
- 100g/4oz softened butter
- 50g/2oz plain flour
- 2 eggs, beaten
- 100g/4oz fresh breadcrumbs
- 6 tbsp vegetable oil

## INGREDIENTS TIP

If salted butter is used for the recipe, just add pepper to season the chicken breasts. Other herbs may be suitable to flavour the garlic butter instead of those suggested – tarragon, thyme and chervil would all work well.

1 Using a sharp knife, cut a small pocket in one side of each of the chicken breasts, being careful not to cut all the way through to the other side.

2 Crush the garlic and grate the lemon zest into a bowl. Pick over the fresh herbs and remove any coarse stalks, as necessary. Finely chop the leaves and add to the bowl. Season with salt and pepper then add the butter and mash together. Shape into a block and wrap in greaseproof paper. Freeze for 30 minutes.

**Step 2**

3 Divide the garlic butter into four and place one in each chicken pocket. Secure the openings with cocktail sticks.

4 Put the flour, the eggs and the breadcrumbs in three separate shallow dishes. Season the chicken and dip first in flour, then in egg, then in breadcrumbs. Dip each piece once more in egg and breadcrumbs. Chill for 2 hours.

**Step 3**

5 Heat the oil in a heavy-based frying pan, add the chicken breasts and fry over moderate heat for about 8 minutes on each side or until golden, crisp and cooked through. Drain on kitchen paper and serve.

**Step 4**

Preparation: **30** Min (plus **2½** Hours freezing and chilling)
Cooking: **16** Min
Per Serving: 487 kcal/2024 kJ;
23g protein; 36g fat;
19g carbohydrate

## TYPICALLY UKRAINIAN

It is said that Kiev is the birthplace of the Russian people. The Ukrainian city was the capital of the first united Russian states and the focal point of this great country. Consequently, its tastes influenced the cuisine of the former empire of the Tsar.

**SERVING SUGGESTION** Potatoes and cabbage are traditional but you may prefer a green salad.

 The Ukrainians would serve tea from a *samovar*, a traditional ornamental kettle.

37

# HUNGARIAN CHICKEN WITH PEPPERS

**HUNGARY**

*Vibrant red peppers are simmered with chicken, stock and white wine in this easy, but exotic, main course. Paprika-flavoured soured cream and yoghurt add the finishing touch.*

## INGREDIENTS
(Serves 4)

- 1.5kg/3lb chicken
- 2 onions
- 1 garlic clove
- 3 red peppers
- 25g/1oz butter
- 1 tbsp vegetable oil
- salt and black pepper
- 150ml/¼ pint hot chicken stock
- 4 tbsp white wine
- 150ml/¼ pint soured cream
- 3 tbsp natural yoghurt
- 1 tbsp paprika

INGREDIENTS TIP

Made from red peppers, paprika is the national spice of Hungary. There are different strengths available, so check labels when you buy. Always buy a small quantity and do not keep for long as it will lose its flavour.

1 Cut the chicken into 8 pieces. Peel and finely chop the onions and the garlic. Cut the peppers in half, take out the seeds and white pith, then chop.

Step 1

2 Melt the butter with the oil in a pan, add the chicken and fry for 10 minutes, turning to brown all over. Remove from the pan. Add the onions and fry for 5 minutes. Add the garlic and peppers and return the chicken to the pan.

Step 2

3 Season with salt and pepper then pour in the chicken stock and white wine. Bring to the boil, reduce the heat to low and cover the pan with a lid. Simmer for about 30 minutes. Mix the soured cream, yoghurt and paprika together in a small bowl. Stir into the liquid in the pan.

4 Turn off the heat, keep the lid on and leave for a further 5 minutes. Serve in the pan you cooked the chicken in or transfer to a warmed serving dish.

Step 3

---

Preparation **20** Min Cooking **50** Min
Per Serving: 626 kcal/2715 kJ;
49g protein; 45g fat;
5g carbohydrate

TYPICALLY HUNGARIAN
Peppers came to Hungary around the 16th century, brought by the Turks who occupied the country. Prized for its beautiful red fruit, the pepper was originally cultivated as an ornamental plant, much the same as potatoes were. Today, Hungary is still famous for its abundant harvest of peppers.

## COOKING TIP

Although you can buy peppers all year round, when they are in season during the summer months they are a lot cheaper. Buy in bulk and freeze: take out the seeds and white pith and coarsely chop. Put into a bowl, pour over boiling water and leave for a few minutes. Drain, cool and freeze for up to 3 months. Use straight from the freezer in casseroles and stews.

## SERVING SUGGESTION

Serve with green beans, tossed in a simple tomato sauce, and boiled potatoes, with butter and parsley.

 A chilled Chardonnay or, if you can find it, a bottle of the famous Hungarian wine, Tokay.

# CHICKEN STUFFED WITH HAM & CHEESE

**SWITZERLAND**

*Tender chicken breasts sandwiched with ham and cheese, then covered with a crisp breadcrumb crust. The cheese melts during cooking and oozes out when you cut into the meat.*

## INGREDIENTS

(Serves 4)

- 4 large chicken breasts, skinned and boned
- salt and black pepper
- 4 slices Gruyère
- 4 slices ham
- 2 tbsp plain flour
- 1 egg
- 100g/4oz dried breadcrumbs
- vegetable oil for deep-fat frying

**TO GARNISH**
- flat leaf parsley sprigs
- 1 lemon

### INGREDIENTS TIP

Gruyère is a great melting cheese and perfect for this dish. Emmenthal, another Swiss cheese, can also be used. Both have a mild taste which becomes fuller flavoured when cooked.

1 Slice the chicken breasts in half and season. Lay the cheese slices onto four pieces, top each with a slice of ham and cover with the remaining chicken halves. Secure with cocktail sticks.

2 Put the flour on a plate. Break the egg into a shallow bowl and beat lightly with a fork. Put the dried breadcrumbs into another shallow bowl.

3 Dip the chicken in the flour and shake off any excess. Dip in the beaten egg then roll in the breadcrumbs, making sure that each chicken piece is completely covered. Pat the crumbs in well.

4 Heat the oil for deep-fat frying to 190°C/375°F. Deep-fry the chicken (in two batches if necessary) for about 8 minutes or until cooked through. Remove from the oil; drain on kitchen paper towels.

5 Leave the parsley sprigs whole or finely chop. Cut the lemon into wedges. Garnish the chicken with the parsley and the lemon wedges.

Step 1

Step 2

Step 4

Preparation **20** Min
Deep-frying **15–20** Min
Per Serving: 402 kcal/1681 kJ;
31g protein; 23g fat;
19g carbohydrate

## TYPICALLY SWISS

From the Gruyère mountains in the French-speaking part of Switzerland comes one of its most famous cheeses. Made since the 12th century, this cow's milk cheese is the mainstay of the classic Swiss *fondue* and *raclette*. Its firm texture and sweet, nutty flavour make it a popular dessert cheese.

## COOKING TIP

To get a really thick, even coating around food to be deep-fried, egg and breadcrumb it twice. Coat once, as in the recipe, put in the fridge and leave for 30 minutes. Dip again in egg and then roll again in the breadcrumbs. Chill for another 30 minutes then deep-fry as instructed.

## SERVING SUGGESTION

Serve with *rösti*, the thick, crunchy 'pancake' of grated potato that originates from Berne, Switzerland.

 Serve with a crisp white wine from either Germany or Italy, such as Pinot Grigio.

**SERVING SUGGESTION** For dessert, serve apple and raisin strudel with a light dusting of icing sugar.

Try a dry white wine, such as Italian Chardonnay or a Spanish Rioja.

# VIENNESE DEEP-FRIED CHICKEN

**AUSTRIA**

## INGREDIENTS

(Serves 4)

- 1.5kg/3lb chicken
- salt
- 100g/4oz plain flour
- 150g/5oz dried breadcrumbs
- 2 eggs
- 3 tbsp milk
- vegetable oil for deep-fat frying

### TO GARNISH

- 1 lemon
- fresh parsley sprigs

### INGREDIENTS TIP

For a really fine coating, coat the chicken in crushed cream crackers instead of the breadcrumbs. Put about 50g/2oz crackers in a bag and crush with a rolling pin. If using another type of cracker, watch the seasoning as some can be quite salty.

*A dish that is simplicity itself: chicken coated in fine breadcrumbs then deep-fried until golden and crisp and served with a classic garnish of lemon and parsley.*

1 Cut the chicken into 12 pieces and then rub all over with salt. Put the flour and the breadcrumbs into two separate shallow bowls. Break the eggs into another shallow bowl and beat with the milk.

2 Dip the chicken pieces in the flour and shake off any excess. Next dip in the egg then roll in the breadcrumbs, patting on the crumbs to make a firm coating.

Step 2

3 Heat the oil for deep-fat frying to 190°C/375°F. Deep-fry the chicken in 3 batches, for about 15 minutes each batch, turning once. The breast portions will need slightly less time – about 12 minutes. As they are fried, put the cooked chicken pieces on a plate lined with kitchen paper towels and keep warm in a low oven.

Step 3

4 Cut the lemon into wedges. Tear the parsley into small sprigs. Garnish the chicken with the lemon wedges and parsley. Alternatively, you can deep-fry the parsley sprigs for a few seconds in the hot oil to make it nice and crisp.

Step 4

Preparation **30** Min Cooking **45** Min
Per Serving: 545 kcal/2279 kJ;
41g protein; 29g fat;
33g carbohydrate

### TYPICALLY AUSTRIAN

Viennese cuisine has its roots firmly planted in the era of the Hapsburg Empire and its most famous dish *Wiener Schnitzel* reflects the Austrian love of crumbed and fried meat. In the city's famous *Naschmarkt* everything is for sale, from wine to wonderful breads.

# 𝒈 WAYS WITH CHICKEN FRICASSEE

*This classic dish of tender chicken in a smooth white sauce enriched with cream is popular in many countries, especially England and France. They add their own favourite ingredients to the basic recipe.*

## BASIC FRICASSEE

**(SERVES 4)**
- 1 carrot
- 1 leek
- 1 celery stalk
- 1 onion
- 1 garlic clove
- 1.5kg/3lb chicken
- fresh parsley
- ½ lemon
- 4 peppercorns
- 1 bay leaf
- salt
- 50g/2oz butter
- 3 tbsp plain flour

*Poaching chicken in stock prevents it drying out.
Cook the chicken, then choose your recipe!*

**1** Bring a large pan of water to the boil. Slice the carrot, leek and celery. Peel the onion and garlic. Add the chicken to the pan, with the prepared vegetables, parsley, lemon, peppercorns, bay leaf and salt. Cover and simmer 45 minutes.

**2** Remove the chicken from pan and cool slightly. Remove meat from bones and dice. For the sauce, melt the butter, add flour and cook for 1 minute. Off the heat, stir in 600ml/ 1 pint of stock. Bring to the boil, stirring, then simmer for 10 minutes.

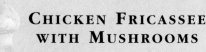

## CHICKEN FRICASSEE WITH MUSHROOMS

Preparation **20** Min Cooking **1½** Hours

### FRANCE

- 225g/8oz button mushrooms
- 225g/8oz shallots
- 25g/1oz butter
- 100ml/4fl oz dry white wine
- 4 tbsp crème fraîche
- salt and black pepper
- fresh chervil

**4** Melt the butter in a pan and fry the shallots for 5 minutes or until golden. Add the wine, bring to the boil and boil rapidly until reduced by half.

**5** Stir the mushrooms, shallots, chicken pieces and crème fraîche into the basic sauce and heat through. Season to taste and serve garnished with the fresh chervil.

**3** Halve mushrooms and peeled shallots.

## CHICKEN FRICASSEE WITH LEMON

Preparation **20** Min Cooking **1½** Hours

USA

- 2 eggs
- ½ lemon
- 4 tbsp single cream
- 1 garlic clove
- pinch of ground ginger
- salt and black pepper
- lemon wedges
- fresh chives

*3* Boil the eggs in water in a pan for 8 minutes. Drain and plunge into cold water. Grate lemon zest and squeeze the juice. Stir into the basic sauce with the chicken and cream. Bring to the boil and simmer for 1 minute.

*4* Crush the garlic and stir into the sauce with the ginger and seasoning. Shell eggs and cut into eighths. Fold into the chicken mixture. Garnish with lemon and fresh chives.

## CHICKEN FRICASSEE WITH ASPARAGUS

Preparation **20** Min Cooking **1½** Hours

### ENGLAND

- 1 bunch asparagus
- 100g/4oz petits pois
- 4 tbsp double cream
- salt and black pepper
- flat leaf parsley

*3* Bring a pan of water to the boil. Meanwhile, cut the asparagus into 4cm/1½in pieces. Add the stalk ends to the pan of boiling water and simmer for 2 minutes. Then add the spear ends and the peas to the pan and simmer for a further 5 minutes.

*4* Drain the asparagus and peas well, then add to the basic sauce with the chicken.

*5* Simmer the sauce for about 1 minute or until everything is heated through. Stir in the double cream and season. Garnish with the parsley.

45

# CHICKEN A LA PROVENÇALE

FRANCE

*A chicken dish that captures all the evocative flavours of the sunny Mediterranean – fragrant fresh herbs, colourful vegetables and aromatic olive oil.*

## INGREDIENTS
(Serves 4)

- 4 chicken breasts, skinned and boned
- 1 tsp dried herbes de Provence
- 2 onions
- 2 garlic cloves
- 1 beefsteak tomato
- 1 aubergine
- 2 courgettes
- 1 red, 1 green and 1 yellow pepper
- 6 tbsp olive oil
- salt and black pepper
- 2 tbsp chopped fresh parsley
- basil leaves

## INGREDIENTS TIP

Available in jars or small bags, herbes de Provence is a mixture of herbs grown in the south of France, usually marjoram, basil, thyme, oregano and often savory.

1 Lay the chicken breasts out flat then rub all over with the herbs. Peel and finely chop the onions and the garlic. Cut the skin of the tomato a few times, put in a bowl and pour over boiling water. Remove the skin and chop the flesh. Coarsely chop the aubergine and the courgettes. Cut the peppers in half, remove the seeds and white pith and cut into wide strips.

Step 1

2 Heat 2 tablespoons of the oil in a large pan, add the chicken breasts and fry for 8 minutes. Turn over and fry for another 5 minutes. Remove from the pan and season well with salt and pepper.

3 Add the onions, garlic, aubergine, courgettes and peppers with the rest of the oil. Fry, stirring, for 10 minutes or until the vegetables have softened. Add the tomato and season with salt and pepper.

Step 1

4 Cover the pan and simmer over low heat for about 10 minutes. Stir in the parsley and put the chicken breasts on top. Cover and simmer for another 10 minutes. Serve the chicken whole or sliced and add to the vegetables. Garnish with the basil leaves.

Step 3

---

Preparation **1** Hour Cooking **35** Min
Per Serving: 445 kcal/1845 kJ;
71g protein; 32g fat;
4g carbohydrate

## TYPICALLY FRENCH
Provence is justly famous not only for its fresh herbs, but also for its garlic and onions. The cold-pressed olive oil from this southern part of France is made from olives that have been allowed to ripen on the trees much longer than usual, giving the oil a fine and distinctive flavour.

## COOKING TIPS

Once the chicken has been returned to the pan of vegetables, make sure you keep the heat down really low, otherwise the vegetables will be overcooked and the chicken will dry out • The skin can be removed before cooking as in the recipe, but leaving the skin on helps to keep the flesh more moist.

## SERVING SUGGESTION

Start with an onion quiche garnished with olives, or grill baguette slices spread with tapenade (olive paste).

A light red wine from southern France, such as Côtes du Lubéron, goes well with chicken.

**S**ERVING **SUGGESTION** For dessert, serve
French apple flan.

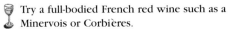 Try a full-bodied French red wine such as a
Minervois or Corbières.

# COQ AU VIN

**FRANCE**

## INGREDIENTS
### (Serves 4)

- 4 chicken leg portions·
- salt and black pepper
- 2 tbsp plain flour
- 2 tbsp sunflower oil
- 25g/1oz butter
- 100g/4oz smoked streaky bacon
- 450g/1lb button onions
- 600ml/1pt red wine
- 1 chicken stock cube
- 2 tbsp tomato purée
- 1 garlic clove
- 1 tbsp chopped fresh thyme or 1 tsp dried
- 225g/8oz mushrooms

### INGREDIENTS TIP

Smoked bacon is quite salty so take care not to over-season the dish. Unsmoked bacon can also be used.

*A classic French casserole of chicken pieces, button onions and mushrooms in a rich red wine sauce. Give your meal a real bistro flavour by serving it with plenty of crusty bread.*

1 Toss the chicken legs in seasoned flour until evenly coated. Heat the oil and butter in a flameproof casserole dish or large frying pan. Add the chicken and fry for 10 minutes, or until browned all over. Remove from the pan and set aside.

2 Cut the bacon into small dice and peel the onions. Add both the bacon and the onions to the casserole or pan and fry for about 5 minutes, stirring occasionally.

3 Pour in the wine and allow to bubble for a minute or two. Then stir in the crumbled stock cube and tomato purée. Crush the garlic and add to the dish or pan with the thyme. Bring to the boil, then return the chicken pieces to the casserole or pan and lower the heat. Cover with a lid and simmer gently for 45 minutes.

4 Halve the mushrooms and add to the dish or pan. Simmer for a further 15 minutes. Adjust the seasoning and serve with slices of French bread.

Step 1

Step 2

Step 3

Preparation: **20** Min
Cooking: **1~1¼ Hours**
Per Serving: 536 kcal/2141 kJ;
22g protein; 32g fat;
30g carbohydrate

## TYPICALLY FRENCH

This dish originated in Burgundy where it was made with local wine and one of the fine-flavoured *poulets de Bresse*. Brandy is often added, and the bread fried in butter until golden. Today coq au vin is eaten all over France and is a popular dish on bistro menus.

# TUSCAN CHICKEN

ITALY

*Tuscany teems with wonderful ingredients – herbs, fresh vegetables, capers and olives – more than enough to turn a humble chicken into this glorious flavour-packed dish.*

## INGREDIENTS

(Serves 4)

- 2 garlic cloves
- 1 sprig fresh rosemary
- 1 tsp black peppercorns
- 1 lemon
- 6 tbsp olive oil
- salt
- 1.5kg/3lb chicken
- 275g/10oz tomatoes
- 1 tbsp tomato purée
- 150ml/¼ pint dry white wine
- 1 sprig fresh sage
- 50g/2oz stoned black olives
- 2 tbsp capers, optional
- sage sprigs, to garnish

INGREDIENTS TIP

The leaves of rosemary sprigs - even fresh ones - can be quite coarse so they need to be finely chopped before adding to a dish.

1 Peel and roughly chop the garlic then pound it together with a few rosemary needles and the peppercorns using a pestle and mortar. Finely grate the zest off the lemon straight into the mortar. Stir in 3 tablespoons of the oil and a pinch of salt.

2 Cut the chicken into 8 pieces. Rub the marinade thoroughly into the chicken and put in a bowl. Tip what's left on top and cover with cling film. Chill for 1 hour. Cut the skin of the tomatoes a few times, put in a bowl and cover with boiling water. Leave for a few minutes, then peel off the skins and cut in half. Set aside.

3 Heat the remaining oil in a large pan and fry the chicken in batches for 10 minutes each batch. Squeeze juice from lemon and mix with tomato purée and wine.

4 Pour the wine mixture into the chicken and stir in the tomatoes. Cover the pan and simmer over low heat for 20 minutes.

5 Chop the rest of the herbs. Cut olives in half and add to the chicken with the chopped herbs and capers, if using. Simmer, covered, for 5 minutes. Garnish with sage.

Step 1

Step 2

Step 5

Preparation 30 Min
Marinating 1 Hour Cooking 35 Min
Per Serving: 576 kcal/2392 kJ;
55g protein; 24g fat;
3g carbohydrate

TYPICALLY ITALIAN

Many dishes from Tuscany are seasoned with capers. The smaller the buds of this native Mediterranean shrub, the more bitter they are. After harvesting, the capers are preserved in brine or vinegar: brine is considered the best option as vinegar tends to overpower their distinctive flavour.

## COOKING TIPS

Make this dish more substantial by adding some
coarsely chopped aubergine and some courgettes
when you add the tomatoes to the chicken • If you
don't have a pestle and mortar, use a small, fairly deep
bowl to hold the ingredients and use the end of a
wooden rolling pin to pound them all together.

## SERVING SUGGESTION

Serve this with a simple leafy green
salad, tossed with vinaigrette flavoured
with fresh herbs.

Serve with a dry white wine from the Tuscan
region, such as a Frascati.

# CHICKEN MADRILEÑO

**SPAIN**

## INGREDIENTS
(Serves 4)

- 16 chicken wings
- 1 sprig fresh rosemary
- salt
- 3 garlic cloves
- ½ tsp paprika
- a few drops of Tabasco
- 100ml/4fl oz dry sherry
- 8 tbsp olive oil
- 3 tbsp chopped fresh parsley
- 275g/10oz dried breadcrumbs
- 3 eggs

### TO GARNISH
- 1 lemon
- flat leaf parsley sprigs

### INGREDIENTS TIP
Spain is the home of sherry, which is often used in cooking. Dry sherry is best in this dish; you could use sweet sherry but the flavour will obviously be different.

*Very crunchy on the outside but juicy and tender inside, these delicious chicken wings are great for parties handed round with drinks when guests arrive.*

1 Using a sharp knife, trim off the wing tips (see Cooking Tip) from the pieces of chicken. Pull the rosemary needles off the sprig and chop finely. Sprinkle the salt over the peeled garlic and crush with the back of a large knife.

2 Combine the rosemary, crushed garlic, paprika, Tabasco and sherry with 2 tablespoons oil. Put the chicken in a bowl and pour over the marinade. Turn the chicken over so it is well coated. Cover; leave for 1 hour, turning occasionally.

3 Add the parsley to the breadcrumbs and mix thoroughly. Break the eggs into a shallow bowl and beat with a fork. Heat the rest of the oil in a large pan.

4 Lift the chicken out of its marinade. Roll in the breadcrumbs, then in the beaten eggs, then again in the breadcrumbs. Shake off any excess coating.

5 Fry the chicken pieces in batches for 20 minutes, turning once. Keep warm in a low oven while you cook the rest. Cut the lemon into wedges. Serve the chicken garnished with lemon and parsley.

Step 1

Step 2

Step 5

Preparation **30** Min
Marinating **1** Hour Cooking **1** Hour
Per Serving: 611 kcal/2584 kJ;
34g protein; 41g fat;
23g carbohydrate

## TYPICALLY SPANISH
The Spaniards' enthusiasm for poultry dates back to the Moorish occupation of almost all of Spain. Not only did the Arabs leave their mark with some beautiful architecture – notably in Andalusia – but they also imparted their love of fried food, and a penchant for chicken, to Spanish culinary traditions.

## COOKING TIPS

Save the wing tips and make some delicious stock.
Put them in a pan, and cover with plenty of water.
Add chopped carrots, leeks and celery and any fresh
herbs you have to hand. Simmer for 3 hours, then
strain and freeze • For a really easy tasty gravy, boil
about 300ml/½ pint of the stock until reduced by
two-thirds, then whisk in a knob of butter to enrich.

## SERVING SUGGESTION

Serve with garlic mayonnaise and
potatoes baked in foil topped with a
spoonful of soured cream.

 A bottle of robust red or white Rioja will go
equally well with this dish.

**SERVING SUGGESTION** Serve with long grain rice, cooked in stock and flavoured with saffron.

Offer a glass of sherry as an aperitif and drink a chilled sparkling rosé with the meal.

# ᴀNDALUSIAN CHICKEN WITH SHERRY

**SPAIN**

## INGREDIENTS

### (Serves 4)

- 1 lemon
- 6 tarragon sprigs
- 2 tbsp olive oil
- 4 chicken breasts, skinned and boned
- salt and black pepper
- 8 shallots, peeled
- 4 garlic cloves, peeled
- 75ml/3fl oz dry sherry
- 150ml/¼ pint chicken stock
- 2 tbsp crème fraîche

INGREDIENTS TIP
Tarragon is said to combine the freshness of mint with the heat of aniseed. It has a fairly intense flavour so add it sparingly to a dish or the other ingredients will be overpowered. If you can't get fresh, use about 1½ teaspoons of dried tarragon instead.

*Tender chicken gently simmered with whole shallots and garlic, in a delicately seasoned sherry and fresh tarragon sauce, finished with tangy crème fraîche.*

1 Using a potato peeler or paring knife, carefully cut the zest off the lemon, making sure you leave all the white pith behind. Cut into thin strips. Squeeze the juice from the lemon and coarsely chop the fresh tarragon.

2 Heat the oil in a large pan. Season the chicken with salt and pepper and add to the pan. Fry for 3 minutes on either side or until browned. Remove from the pan. Add the shallots and garlic and fry over moderate heat for about 5 minutes, stirring.

3 Stir in the lemon zest, tarragon, sherry and chicken stock. Stir well, scraping up any bits from the bottom of the pan. Season and stir in 1 tablespoon lemon juice. Bring to the boil; return the chicken to the pan.

4 Reduce the heat to low, cover the pan and simmer for 15 minutes. Remove the chicken from the pan; cut into thick slices and keep warm. Stir the crème fraîche into the sauce and bring back to the boil. Boil rapidly until reduced and thickened. Season again. Serve the chicken with the sauce.

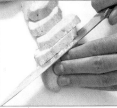

Step 2

Step 4

Step 4

---

Preparation **20** Min Cooking **30** Min
Per Serving: 282 kcal/1180 kJ;
34g protein; 14g fat;
1g carbohydrate

TYPICALLY SPANISH
Sherry acquired its name from the small Andalusian town of Jerez de la Frontera. The young wine is matured in oak barrels for a year, then fortified with brandy. Next, it is carefully blended to produce a range of dry, medium and sweet sherries.

# CHICKEN PIRI-PIRI

*Almost Portugal's national dish, this chicken sauté with wine is flavoured with fiery chillies, peppers, piquant black olives and a generous sprinkling of fresh parsley.*

## INGREDIENTS
(Serves 4)

- 4 chicken breasts, skinned and boned
- 2 garlic cloves
- 2 red chillies
- 2 red peppers
- 3 tbsp olive oil
- 200ml/7fl oz dry white wine (eg Vinho Verde)
- 100g/4oz black olives
- salt and black pepper
- fresh parsley

### INGREDIENTS TIP

Vinho Verde, or green wine, comes from the lush northern regions of Portugal and it is the wine 25 per cent of its population choose to drink. Low in alcohol, it has a dry, tangy but refreshing flavour. Try a French Muscadet if you can't find it.

1 Cut the chicken breasts into thin strips. Finely chop the garlic. Cut the chillies and peppers in half, remove the seeds and all the white pith. Cut both into thin strips.

2 Heat half the oil in a large pan, add the chicken strips and stir-fry over high heat, stirring all the time, for a couple of minutes or until browned. Remove the chicken from the pan and set aside.

3 Add the rest of the oil to the pan, add the garlic, chillies and peppers and fry for 3 minutes or until softened. Add the wine and bring to the boil. Return the chicken to the pan, add the olives and season with salt and pepper. Reduce the heat to moderately low, cover the pan and simmer for 15 minutes.

4 While the chicken is cooking, remove the stems from the parsley and finely chop the leaves. Chop either on a board with a large knife, or in a mug using a pair of kitchen scissors. Sprinkle the chicken with the parsley and serve.

Step 1

Step 3

Step 4

Preparation **15** Min Cooking **25** Min
Per Serving: 346 kcal/1444 kJ;
34g protein; 19g fat;
2g carbohydrate

### TYPICALLY PORTUGUESE

Piri-piri are the small red, extremely hot chillies that are so popular in Portugal and used to flavour everything from seafood to poultry. There is also a fiery pepper sauce marketed under the same name: you will find a bottle of piri-piri on the table in most restaurants in Portugal to spice up your food.

## COOKING TIP
If you love the heat of chillies, keep the seeds in and they will impart even more fiery flavour. On the other hand, if you prefer a milder taste, either remove the seeds and white pith and chop the flesh as in this recipe, or simply leave them whole, then remove from the sauce just before serving.

## SERVING SUGGESTION
Start with a plate of fried small fish such as sardines or whitebait and some fresh crusty bread.

The Vinho Verde used in the dish is also just right to drink with this meal.

# GREEK CHICKEN WITH LEMONS

*You can almost taste the sunshine in this simple dish of chicken browned in olive oil, then simmered with vegetables and sharp, tangy lemons.*

## INGREDIENTS

(Serves 4)

- 1.5kg/3lb chicken
- 2 lemons
- 1 onion
- 2 carrots
- 2 celery stalks
- 3 tbsp olive oil
- salt
- pinch cayenne pepper
- 150ml/¼ pint vegetable stock
- fresh parsley

INGREDIENTS TIP

When buying lemons, choose fruit that feel heavy for their size as these will be the most juicy. To extract the maximum amount of juice, use at room temperature and roll on a work surface with the palm of your hand before squeezing out the juice.

1 Cut the chicken into 12 pieces. Using a potato peeler or paring knife, carefully cut off the lemon rind, then cut into thin strips. Squeeze the juice from both lemons.

2 Peel and finely chop the onion. Peel the carrots and trim the celery, reserving the green leaves. Slice the carrots and celery.

3 Heat the oil in a pan with a tight fitting lid. Add the chicken pieces and fry over high heat for 8 minutes on each side, until golden. Remove the chicken from the pan. Add the onion, carrots and celery to the pan and fry for 5 minutes. Return the chicken and season with salt and cayenne pepper.

4 Stir the lemon rind and lemon juice into the vegetable stock and stir into the pan. Finely chop 2 tablespoons parsley and half the celery leaves and stir into the chicken. Reduce the heat to low, cover the pan and simmer for another 30 minutes.

5 Pick off another 1 tablespoon parsley leaves and chop with the rest of the celery leaves. Use to garnish the dish.

Step 1

Step 2

Step 4

---

Preparation **45** Min Cooking **50** Min
Per Serving: 539 kcal/2244 kJ;
45g protein; 39g fat;
1g carbohydrate

TYPICALLY GREEK

Lemons grow in abundance throughout Greece, particularly on the islands of Naxos and Sifnos where they thrive under the brilliant blue skies and warm climate. A lemon liqueur, a speciality of the islands, is produced from the surplus fruit.

## COOKING TIP

To make the job of paring off the lemon rind easier, buy yourself a canelle knife (sometimes called a lemon zester). As you pull it over the surface of the lemon, it takes the rind off in thin neat strips, thus saving you the time-consuming task of peeling off the rind in large pieces, then cutting into thin strips.

## SERVING SUGGESTION

A loaf of fresh white crusty bread makes an easy accompaniment, or serve with rice or pasta.

 Serve the meal with Retsina or Demestica, and offer a glass of Metaxa brandy at the end.

# TURKISH CHICKEN PILAF

**TURKEY**

## INGREDIENTS
### (Serves 4)

- 4 chicken breasts, skinned and boned
- 1 large onion
- 2 garlic cloves
- 225g/8oz tomatoes
- 1 small aubergine
- 1 courgette
- 1 red pepper
- 3 tbsp vegetable oil
- ½ tsp saffron powder
- 150ml/¼ pint chicken stock
- 1 dried chilli
- 40g/1½oz currants
- 225g/8oz long grain rice
- salt and black pepper
- ½ tsp ground cumin

### TO GARNISH
- chopped fresh parsley

### INGREDIENTS TIP
Basmati is the finest long grain rice and best for a pilaf. Rinse before cooking to remove excess starch.

*Pilaf is served all over Turkey, and can be anything from a simple dish of rice fried in butter to a more lavish version like this with chicken, dried fruit and colourful vegetables.*

1 Cut the chicken into 2.5cm/1 inch cubes. Peel and chop the onion and garlic. Slit the tomato skins, cover with boiling water, leave for a few minutes, then peel and dice. Cut the aubergine and courgette into small pieces. Deseed and chop the pepper.

2 Heat the oil in a pan, add the chicken, onion, garlic, aubergine, courgette and pepper and fry over high heat for about 4 minutes, stirring all the time. Stir the saffron into the stock with 450ml/¾ pint water, then pour into the pan. Bring to the boil.

3 Crumble the dried chilli, add to the pan and stir in the currants, rice and tomatoes. Season with salt, pepper and cumin. Reduce the heat to low, cover the pan and simmer for about 20-25 minutes, stirring now and again and adding more water if necessary.

4 Finely chop the parsley – you will need about 2 tablespoons. Spoon the pilaf into a serving dish and sprinkle with the chopped parsley.

**Step 1**

**Step 3**

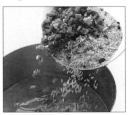

**Step 3**

Preparation **20** Min Cooking **25** Min
Per Serving: 560 kcal; 2354 kJ;
39g protein; 25g fat;
49g carbohydrate

### TYPICALLY TURKISH
*Raki*, a spirit distilled from grapes or figs and aniseed, is a great favourite in Turkey. Like the French *pastis*, it is served diluted with icy cold water which makes it cloudy. As well as to drink, Turkish men gather in the coffee houses to smoke the large ornate water pipes called *narghiles*.

**SERVING SUGGESTION** Serve with mixed salad and yoghurt with chopped cucumber and herbs.

Serve iced tea or *ayran*, chilled yoghurt whisked with iced water and a little salt.

61

# DICTIONARY OF TERMS

*An A to Z of the more unusual ingredients and cooking terms used throughout this book.*

## BAMBOO SHOOTS

Available in cans, these add crunchiness and a mild sweet-savoury flavour to stir-fries and other oriental dishes.

## BEAN SPROUTS

The crisp, curly white shoots of the mung bean, bean sprouts add bulk and nutritious crunch to stir-fries. They can also be steamed and sprinkled with soy sauce to serve as a vegetable, or blanched and added to salads.

## CHERVIL

A pretty herb with a mild aniseed flavour, chervil is an essential part of the French *fines herbes* mix. The flavour is destroyed by heat so use in cold dishes or as a garnish.

## CHILLI SAUCE

Chilli sauces play a lively part in the cooking of both East and West. Tabasco, the best-known American hot pepper sauce now has a green cousin made from the milder Jalapeño pepper. Chilli sauces are used not just in cooking but also as a table condiment to spice up cooked food, and hot sweet varieties can be almost as thick as ketchup.

## COATING

This means turning food in something dry to form a crust and keep juices in during cooking. The lightest of coatings is a simple dusting in seasoned flour before food is shallow-fried. For sturdier coating, food is dipped in flour, beaten egg and breadcrumbs before being deep-fried.

## FISH SAUCE

Thai cooking relies heavily on *nam pla*, a clear, dark brown savoury sauce made from salted and fermented fish. Other south-east Asian cuisines have similar sauces, including the Chinese oyster sauce.

---

## CHOOSING AND PREPARING CHICKEN

The more naturally a bird is raised the better it will taste.

*Cornfed* – these yellow-fleshed birds have been fed on corn for at least part of their lives but will have been intensively reared unless the label states 'free-range'.

*Free-range* – this indicates a barn-raised bird that has day-time access to outdoor runs and natural vegetation for at least half its life.

*Traditional free-range* – will have been raised in smaller flocks, allowed more outdoor space and more time to reach maturity.

*Free-range total freedom* – indicates high welfare standards and birds of a traditional breed from smaller farms.

### Cutting a chicken into pieces

*Chickens can be jointed into two breasts, two wings and two legs (6 pieces) which can be separated into thighs and drumsticks (8 pieces) or each part halved (12 pieces). It is cheaper to buy a whole chicken and joint it yourself but you can buy chicken joints to the total weight you need if you prefer.*

### Here's how....

*Most butchers will do this for you but it's really easy to joint the chicken yourself: stand the bird, domed breastbone up on a wipe clean surface and cut each leg away from the body. Use kitchen scissors to cut along the breastbone and divide the carcass in half. Cut away breast sections then the wings. Remove the wing tips and save with the carcass for stock. Now cut into the number of pieces you want: cooking times are less the smaller the pieces are.*

## THE RIGHT PANS

Using the correct pan for stove-top cooking ensures success.

### Frying Pan

*The best frying pans are heavy-based to hold the heat evenly and avoid warping. You can also fry chicken pieces golden without any fat in a heavy or non-stick pan. Pans that come with lids are useful too.*

### Wok

*Woks are made of thin metal that gets hot quickly. Heat without fat then add the oil and flavourings before adding the main ingredients. Cut everything into small pieces before you start – cooking time is minimal and food is kept moving throughout. For this reason woks are deep, to stop food jumping over the side, and the best ones have a long handle so that you can toss the contents by shaking the pan.*

### Cooking Methods in the Wok

*As well as stir-frying, the wok makes an excellent vessel for deep-frying. A wok with a lid can be used for braising and has a rack or basket for steaming.*

## GINGER

Available as a powdered spice, used in desserts and baking, or fresh as a knobbly root which adds spicy sweetness to savoury cooking. Break off a piece, peel then grate or finely chop.

## MARINADE

Usually contains oil and something acidic like vinegar or lemon juice. Food is marinated to tenderise and add flavour prior to cooking. There are also dry marinades of spices.

## PILAF

An Indian or Middle Eastern dish of rice cooked in water or stock with other ingredients, sometimes enough to make a complete main course, otherwise just flavoured with whole and ground spices and butter to serve as a side dish. It can also be baked in the oven.

## SESAME OIL

A strongly flavoured oil made from sesame seeds, it is used in tiny amounts as a dressing and to give a nutty aroma to cooked food.

## SESAME SEEDS

Chinese and Japanese cooks toast the seeds by shaking them in a dry pan over heat, then scatter them over noodles, fish or other soft food as a crunchy garnish. In the Middle East, the untoasted seeds are ground into a paste called *tahina* that is used in dressings and is an important ingredient of *hummus*.

## SOY SAUCE

As integral to the cooking of the Far East as salt is to ours (and often fulfilling a similar function), soy sauce comes in dark and light varieties. It's important to buy a properly fermented product, preferably a Japanese soy sauce (called *shoyu*) which can be bought from larger supermarkets – light soy has a milder flavour than dark.

## STIR-FRYING

A very fast cooking method for foods usually eaten with chopsticks rather than a knife and fork. Ingredients are cut into small pieces before cooking, then added to hot, flavoured oil – meat and hard root vegetables first, followed by leafy vegetables. Liquids are added last to make a little coating sauce. Ingredients are kept moving during cooking, which makes a deep-sided wok the best shaped pan for stir-frying.

## TORTILLA

Pancake-thin wheat or cornmeal breads of Mexico. They are either soft for wrapping around meat and salads, or crisp U-shapes, or tacos, to contain the filling. Widely available from all supermarkets.

# INDEX

## Acknowledgements

**Picture Credits**
**All cover and recipe pictures:**
International Masters Publishers BV/International Masters Publishers Ltd
Food Photography: Eising, Dorothee Gödert, Peter Rees, Manuel Schnell,
Neil Mersh, Philip Wilkins
**Agency pictures:**
*Introduction:* Look: Heeb, page 5 top left; Tony Stone: Allison, page 4, bottom
right; DeVore, page 5 top left, Everts, page 5 bottom right, Huber, page 4/5
bottom middle
*Pictures for the Typically sections:* Anthony Blake: page 8, 46, 49
Cephas: Blythe, page 12; Kielty, page 43; Rock, page 55
Comstock: page 14
Garden Picture Library: Viard, page 56; Lamontagne, page 50
Robert Harding: page 23, 30; Frerck, page 28, 32
Hutchison: Egan, page 36
Food Matters: Eriksson, page 20
Impact: Cormack, page 38; Edwards, page 6; Fear, page 18
Harry Smith Collection: page 11

Measuring Ingredients
Tsp = teaspoon, Tbsp = tablespoon
Teaspoons and tablespoons are level and are measured using standard
measuring spoons.
Follow either metric or imperial measurements; don't mix the two.

Tony Stone: page 42; Armand, page 24; Hiser, page 26; Sitton, page 50;
Tweedie, page 31
Telegraph Colour Library: Moss, page 58; The Stock Directory, page 56
With special thanks to David Mellor for supplying props
© International Masters Publishers BV/International Masters Publishers Ltd
MCMXCVIII
Reproduced by Rapida and Studio One Origination, London, UK
Printed in Italy by Mondadori